Advance Praise for
What Comes from the Night

Along the banks of the Loire River, the shorelines of the Quiberon peninsula in the Atlantic, or amidst the yellow wildflowers in the Alpine Garden on Mount Cenis, John Taylor's masterful poems show us how to trust in the seeable world. At once images and mirages, Taylor's portraits move perceptively forward with due diligence among "hints of history," whether they are somersaulting pebbles or "wings riddled with wormholes." These meditations invite the reader to peer with the poet into the "tiny secret lives" of the landscape before him, reminiscent of the quiet clarity of Kobayashi Issa. Indeed, Taylor's "you" is inclusive, opening a window where one can, like a child for the first time, spot the "rabbit through the hedge" of an always-separate world. When you enter into these poems, crouched "in a lean-to under dead branches" your mind lets itself go and asks, Why have I not always rested here?

    — Katie Lehman, author of *Emily Dickinson's Lexicon*

Despite their visual aspect, these extraordinary poems are not fragments. Paradoxically, though crystals in the conciseness of their meaning, they are wildflowers culled from a moment's awareness, and pressed between a notebook's leaves. John Taylor recomposes these instants without exalting them: he achieves a verbal ascesis, the music of restraint.

    — Hoyt Rogers, author of *Thresholds* and *Sailing to Noon*

As if on his first day on earth, with the eyes of a child and a man of ancient times, John Taylor writes by listening to a mystery that lives in each thing. His gaze is beckoned by moments in which things are no longer themselves and at the same time not yet something else: it is the enchantment of transmutation, of the multiple transitions through which day becomes night, darkness becomes light, and the miracle of life comes true.

> — Franca Mancinelli, author of *All the Eyes that I Have Opened* and *The Butterfly Cemetery*

Reading John Taylor's *What Comes from the Night* is what it feels like to not just be part of the universe, to not just deeply explore it, observe it, name its many aspects or live under its conditions, but rather to merge with all of its particulars, accepting the reality of who we were before being conscious, who we are now while being conscious, and who we'll always be after this kind of consciousness has passed. Through the beauty and simplicity of Taylor's language, we're comforted realizing that we've always been alive, that we continue to live and will go on living as part of life's circular nature. However, to accomplish this life is not through any beginning or end but is rather through a desire to show how things so opposed to each other, which usually avoid each other, which cancel each other out or eventually shrink into each other's oblivion unresolved, not only attract each other, but join this circle and deepen where each's hidden roots mingle no matter their outward appearance or place in time.

> — Paul B. Roth, author of *Weightless Earth* and *Moments in Place*

WHAT COMES FROM THE NIGHT

Also by John Taylor

What Comes from the Night

Poems

John Taylor

COYOTE ARTS

Library of Congress Control Number: 2024941819

ISBN   Paper   978-1-58775-052-6
       E-Book   978-1-58775-053-3

3 5 7 9 10 8 6 4 2

Coyote Arts LLC
PO Box 6690
Albuquerque, New Mexico 87197-6690
www.coyote-arts.com

Contents

Keeping Faith
with the Mother Tongue

John Taylor, above all a poet, has a formidable *arrière-pays* in the shape of his work as a distinguished literary critic and major translator. His own poetry and short stories form the apex of a triangle of powerful forces whose base could have but doesn't overshadow the poetry. At the base of the triangle are translations of and essays on visionary poets of quality and power such as Jacques Dupin and Philippe Jaccottet, who serve as invisible witnesses to his quest. To venture forth on a journey of one's own into a landscape which is at once mental and physical, parallel to those of his French poets, requires humility and tough-mindedness. I see John Taylor as a latter-day Casper David Friedrich, apparently alone in his personal space, but taking readers (including the invisible witnesses) along with him ("you") to the apex of "the mind [with its] mountains" (Hopkins). Taylor's diction and syntax are filtered throughout, pure and cleansed of his earlier and surely benign influences, so that the poetry shall master the temptations of the surrounding powers. Furthermore, the reader's ear picks up on the personal tonality and sonority: his rhythms (including always necessary and "natural" enjambments) are an outlier for readers young and old, again transcending various remote origins in Williams,

Imagism, French and other European poets. The introjected landscape is rural and sometimes Alpine, without succumbing to the lure of pastoral. A rare parallel—affinity with no influence in either direction—might be the Lawrentian flower poems of a younger English contemporary of Dupin, Jon Silkin. John Taylor, resident for most of his adult life in the French countryside and in the language of its inhabitants, keeps faith with his mother tongue. As he writes in this beautiful book: "to bear endings / find your bearings / in beginnings."

— Anthony Rudolf, author of
Silent Conversations and *European Hours: Collected Poems*

the palm of your hand
restraining water
or hindering wind

or when you gather twigs
for flames

these are clues

Endings and Beginnings

I.

with a wish you opened a door
later closed by a breeze
gently
as if it knew

John Taylor

you've sown seeds too long
in your secret garden
where the seasons
take no turns

*

sometimes at rapids
already the islets, the sandbars,
the slow flow away,
the evaporation

*

what from afar seemed a furrow
traced by a plowshare
was a ravine
rocky, waterless, also a mirage

now a wind blows:
the ripe fruit falls, rots,
enriches soil less and less yours
in every one of your orchards

      *

slight yet significant
the distance grows
until you withdraw
into the other ending

John Taylor

mere hints here
of what happened before,
during, after—
weak words instead of

II.

silently you suffer
inside a silence
you've made to measure
on every other silence

     *

you grope for a handhold,
a foothold: this recurrent cliff
you cannot unroll
into a field

it's not only that wind
blows against you:
it shifts;
there can be no wind

        *

even if something grows
where sunlight broods the soil
soft like a whisper
you must move on

III.

to bear endings
find your bearings
in beginnings

*

each answer wells, hidden
in the grass, a trickle,
a new question seeking air

a rare wind taps, taps
throughout the night,
then gold shimmers
on the shutter

*

after the storm you rake
the autumn;
between the last leaves
the grass glistens

*

a mere root
in your days,
you are warmed
and surface

your enigmas—for once
you scatter them
without sweeping them back
into circles

*

your eyes are touched
by a passing thought
that stops,
enters your blood

*

first hatchings:
bits of eggshell,
fluffy down in the nest,
already keepsakes

wet birch leaves
on the ground: dance steps
in next realm

*

as when in childhood you spotted
a rabbit through the hedge
that separated two worlds

wandering thoughts, wasps
appear, circle, vanish,
bats dart through the twilight,

swallows dip, soar—
each one knows;
we all know

      *

a dark golden flare, a word
swims up, dives
to where it must go

you must go
a dark golden flare
you can begin writing these poems

Sandbar

as the river rises,
what is stable
though of sand and silt
remains longer
than you had thought

                                  watch

this limit

that passing terns know

Seascape

again an island
where you bedded bones
on granite

*

the clouds reply
with their journey

no *why* stops them

*

accept this,
their coming into being, into form,
their homecoming

down here you watch:

                       out there

the island seems to drift;
the ocean, to lose its shimmer

       *

the shadow covering you
like a dark sheet
awakens you
into the night
that hasn't come

In Memory Of

a tree trying to take root
in the chilly air
while you sit on a branch
in its crown
along the wet ground
and breathe deeply

John Taylor

another tree stands
on the same muddy bank
the surrogate shore

the trembling reflection
of its needles in backwater
seems more permanent
than this rough bark
upon which you rest your hand

but now you wonder

which can guide you—
your finger pointing at ripples
or your callous palm

nothing but ashes scattered
in the bay
you will never sit on that shore

these ashes in your mouth
full of saliva

if you spit on the ground
maybe some thistle will sprout
its spray of blue

        *

not-yet-last words fade
another voice explains
hangs up

you wait for the second call
that never comes
yet has in fact come through
with your own variants
for more than a decade

silence that is no longer sleep
nor the width of the ocean
the continent between

perhaps what you heard
during all those centuries

indeed try to remember
what you listened to
for millennia
before you were born

there is this hollowness
that cannot hold
enough solace for you
cannot soothe and shelter

yet it is also as if
this hollowness were not
what you think it is
or would like it to be

should not be enclosed
were not enclosed

were instead
a hollowness
that cannot hold

another origin
returns to the seawater
the grave
that is no grave

and the specks fall
to the sandy firmament
from which something might
burrow down
or rise
through the liquid darkness
to root in the air

Backwater

backwater over clayish mud:
the edges of your body
spread, vanish
as the other water rises

or they shrink, vanish
among the carp, the waterlilies,
the knotweed

wait

accept

John Taylor

one levee seems to hold
forever;
the others shift in every instant

everything essential
perhaps flows in parallel,
on the other side;

you are here, with time

in your lymph:
it's a matter of slope
and passage

drops, droplets
from ash leaves and bramble thorns:
their music becomes yours

limbs are lintels
thresholds to the sky

sparkles
on your brackish skin

now and then the river floods
through the wound

this is when you lie down
among the comfrey healing bones,
the tansies with their bitter buttons
of gold

what you see of yourself
in the tern's gaze
is darker than dead bark
and it gleams

peer ahead:
make your own eyes now
ponds of birth

Swiftwater

I.

snow sparkles
in the air
in the one
life
outside the window

*

your thoughts join the real
flurries
on the dark branch

all now one
for one moment

*

the gusts then bring
the scintillating beyond
to your eyelids

to where you crouch
near water streaming down
between snowy banks

John Taylor

II.

lines of ice cracking
on the lake

calling out
from Dante's hell

    *

ice and warmth
touching yielding
in the day speeding away

III.

through a lattice of boughs
you spot Venus's lantern
the distant sleigh
of the nearby night

    *

now you can journey
now you can measure and accept
the soft invisible contours
the swift water resisting ice

The Bessans Notebook

the candelabrum of snow is broken
two candles are missing

the hand at the summit
no longer cups
no longer soothes

*

instead of light in the cradling palm
mere fingers of melting snow

you wonder if the watery nails
scratch away gently

the rock abandons its grip
abandons itself
drops

*

stone surfaces reassert themselves
face the fire
face you
across the valley

you were up there once
where ice glistens
in the first light

more must collapse
inside outside

but will the scree be covered
by quick water slowing
by wild grasses swaying

        *

behind the haze
is what must become

wisps of fog over last bits of lasting snow

the snow-sprinkled silhouette emerges
against the sun

at least a line up there
can be grasped

glacial water flowing through the notch

hollow out a threshold in yourself

John Taylor

cascades from the same source
long separate in their solitary rush to the encounter

what descends seeks a wider flow
dissolution
each strand unravels in the warp

aim your eye at what weaves
unweaves

      *

the mountain knows shadows greater than itself

its glacier is hanging by a thread of ice
you too must go through your eye

where shadows of clouds roll like waves over the slopes
muscles of earth

a monticule caresses a shoulder

the northern slope has sources that you need
they sparkle in shadow
as if feting some pure joy
in giggles and whispers
that reach down like hands

     *

familiar paths
on which memories
are reminders

beyond the banks of the Arc
the pale-yellow pasture stands out against the mountains

one by one the summits drape their darkness over what follows
as if initiating

sometimes a high sheen of grass retains its gold
as if hesitating to be put to sleep
then it too merges with all the evenings

      *

no refuge
what seem caves are shadows
cast by gaps and bulges
yet dark green tufts
sprout from cracks

no sheer cliff
if you look closely

      *

sit down beneath
the water seeping from the rock face

at night think of cooling words

uttered long ago between these branches
where piled-up stones mark the trail
across floodwater silt

and the Arc flows within your blindness
a clicking and clacking as pebbles somersault

this music is yours

　　　*

the naked water
the naked stone over which it flows

if you were this

you pick up a rock

it has dropped through your life
to the present moment

bring it closer to your lips

or a stream-soaked branch left behind

let it steady you

      *

as you walk away
what the curly dock flowers must know
already comforts

their dark torches light a way

Yellow Wildflowers

Portraits

you, the muted glow
of a source—
but now you must
let your sap sink,
protect yourself

in your collapse you become
what is left over
in the darkest soil
to grow hands again,
to open them

the crack in the rock
you cannot close up,
only fill it with yourself:
steady, verdant, rising,
lifting

a shy stone not shying away—
yet you are no stone
but a flower,
a bird,
the track of a bird

your glance sends out a runner
over poor soil; it roots,
blooms, sends out another
to run further,
each time rooting

John Taylor

like soft sage, this milky
down on your stems,
your waiting
for buds to burst
out of your calyxes

shyly you put forth
petals so golden
they soothe,
promise
deep succulent darkness

you place your radiance
in front of you, shielding
your flesh, or some secret,
at every wayside
where you take shelter

the droplets you hold
you do not hold out,
jewels in a concave case,
ever wary
of someone else's thirst

you never tear off
your see-through blinders, even
when true love nears,
nor when
love nears and is false

you bring bright stars
to the speckled sunlight
until the lacework of arms
welcomes other shadows,
shields smothering you

your nipple-like buds,
your leaves a naked back
moving away, falling
from someone's
yellow afternoon

at your core a butterfly
who seeks not to be
as you are: a cluster of white,
rooted in scree
from the onset

whenever you hear
endearing names
of nibbling and fleeing,
your mouse-ears open,
your hawk-wings spread

from your innermost whorl
you sow yourself
into indifferent winds,
arbitrary descents,
finalities of foreign ground

overlooked, neglected,
you grow,
tied to invisible trellises,
weaving yourself up
and out of entanglements

unseen and when seen
unheeded until your mouth
frees its tongue, frees
its tiny sounds: now you are
an orchid in high grass

vanquishing your restraint,
you find the words
to be yourself, to unroll
your song, make
cradles of this brisk air

you are the nameless flower
of coincidence:
a shadow lingers,
the path turns,
and you gleam

What Comes from the Night

from the yellow notebook on the bedside table

never a breath of wind
across these fields
yet you lean
into something
like wind

    *

when the real wind blows
through leaves your answers
branch into questions

John Taylor

the muddy trail
at times a torrent
down through scorched pastures

up you climb
through life and desiccation

up or down
deepens into a ditch
carved by a torrent
whose roar remains

      *

it's past midnight near the stream
where already you know
an impossible animal
from the slope
will be grazing
or lying in wait
near what matters

      *

you stare at the darkest spots
until the dim stars emerge
as your teacher said they would

as when one turns away
from a horizon

your dream withdraws

over meadows
over hills
into woods

        &

and from woods
from a clearing

your dream slips off

between tree trunks
faint birdcalls trails
narrowing
to tiny secret lives

John Taylor

later than usual you awake
after running through woods
and turning left or right
onto other paths

as if nothing depended

       *

in front of the stone well
you cast an arc
with your flashlight

you are searching for something
you have dropped inside

yet grope for it
within a memory of light

the music lingers behind your eyes
reverberates from the empty source
until you open them
to any other material thing

*

of everything you have scattered
has a little of it gathered elsewhere
survived somehow
in some other night

whatever the answer
you have not learned
to listen to this night

John Taylor

your search for forgotten words
leads you into an absence
you try to reach again
once the words are remembered

you notch the dark edge
stand back up

the puddle
trickles away
with your face

    *

drizzle on seeded soil

dull days
full of change

    *

all the dead branches stacked up
to make a lean-to
under which you'd like to crouch

John Taylor

shape out an arch
in the tangle of branches

the beginning of the next trail
will be your home

try to be twig
or waterdrop

and may the mud soothe

smooth over
the yielded footstep

a sleepless darkness
presses down on you
like a thick fallen branch

you close your eyes

a bed of light-colored twigs

*

a small stone
for a pillow

warm dry breezes
rub up against your eyes

yet outside
nothing stirs

the imaginable endings
and still others
are blowing within you

*

there is a stone
smooth or unsmooth
split or unsplit

or a thicket
with a shelter
or not

John Taylor

something settles
like lichen
on your innermost bark

and its sheen
in whatever light
is jeweled
like a waterdrop

      *

don't spell out too quickly
this silence inside you

an uprooted tree
below this cliff

the rootlets quiver
in the remaining wind
that you also are

                    *

you're haunted by leaps
the last second in the air

                    *

the end initiates

John Taylor

so far from what springs
splashes over rocks
greens the parched field

so far
from the enigma

                    *

coming from childhood into your hands
a leaf boat for the rivulet
trickling over toppled twigs

between shadow and brightness
you cannot see the line
and lose your way
in the sunniest opening
darkened by your own foliage

*

it's only nightfall this time
not the nightfall inside you

John Taylor

when seeds and sprouts
bring no joy
remember the robin

    *

at the mere thought
of another source
you withdraw
from the trickle
the moist moss
the damp leafy topsoil
the dew on the moldy branches

    *

rocks logs
holding back the stream
that flows through every one of your days

and you have rolled them there

will you unfold
or fold yourself back up

too wary too venturesome
the wren in the sunlight
at the edge of the dark bush

*

fingerprints of light
on the wall of the woods

or hands of darkness
behind every oak

*

you keep closing your eyes
to watch the same memory
with timorous expectancy
even if you know
the other ending

just the light on these blades
of chive
their thin line of life
like some words together

John Taylor

a brief bee
in the pear blossom

both ready

    *

an empty seedpod
taken as a whole
offers its wholeness

    *

your time as sap
sleeping in the bud

and you flower
to fall
to rise

    *

you grope for whatever
the dream might have left

pattering
on the lean-to
of pages

Fragments of my days, saved from my nights, prolong my nights.
Fragmentos de mis días, salvados de mis noches, prolongan mis noches.
—*Antonio Porchia*

From What was Given

from what was given:
a shield, a sword

    unknown knight

from what was given:
a cloak, a cross

    unknown knight

from what was given:
your eyes
remain uneffaced

    Thibault de Bretagne

To an Angel Depicted on a Reliquary

again lifeless in the cloak
they wove and you wonder—
will you ever cast it off

the only direction splits like a hair
the angle widens

John Taylor

when you glance sideways
your knife-eye sharpens
initiates you

the spilled blood on the ground
for what other sacrifices

you spot an oak leaf
recalling the palm
or is it the pain
of a mother's hand
that no longer retains

when you leave the line
will you leave behind
your leave-taking

what you turn away from—
will it reemerge
as the finality
of every new destination

John Taylor

the tiny flame of questions—
when you point it elsewhere
it begs
only your darkness

in the end your right foot decides
throws you off balance
to help you stumble
into flight

John Taylor

a blank gray sky before spring
the river has risen
to the top of the levee

you look at your wings
riddled with wormholes
you have flown through the earth

Notes & Acknowledgments

Endings and Beginnings: some of these poems were first published in *The Bitter Oleander* (Vol. 27, No. 2, Autumn 2021).

Sandbar: the imagery is inspired by the Loire River as it flows past the village of La Bohalle.

Seascape: written from a high point on the Quiberon peninsula overlooking the Atlantic Ocean.

In Memory Of: the imagery of the first and last poems of this sequence allude to a remark by the philosopher Simone Weil: "L'arbre est en vérité enraciné dans le ciel." This perspective was called to my attention by the Italian poet Franca Mancinelli, who uses Weil's words as one of the epigraphs to her book *Libretto di transito,* which I translated as *The Little Book of Passage* (The Bitter Oleander Press, 2018). This sequence was published in *The Fortnightly Review* (11 January 2024), accompanied by the drawings of the British artist Sam Forder.

Backwater: the imagery is inspired by some backwater of the Loire River near a right-bank beach and marshy area called "La Belle Poule." This sequence was selected for the international *Artists for Plants* project at the Svalbard Global Seed Vault in Norway in October 2022 and was used in the film produced for this same project.

John Taylor

Swiftwater: these poems were written in the village of Metabief, in the French Jura.

The Bessans Notebook: these poems and fragments were written in the Alpine village of Bessans, in the Haute Maurienne, and in the surrounding mountains. This sequence was first published in *The Bitter Oleander* (Vol. 27, No. 2, Spring 2021).

Yellow Wildflowers: each "portrait" is inspired by a specific yellow wildflower. Because these flowers were found and identified in France, and in some cases in the Franco-Italian Alpine Garden on Mount Cenis, I am adding the common French and Italian names:

"you, the muted glow. . ."
> *birthwort (aristolochia clematitis)* / aristoloche clématite / aristolochia clematite

"in your collapse you become. . ."
> *st. john's wort (hypericum perforatum)* / millepertuis perforé / erba di san giovanni

"the crack in the rock. . ."
> *austrian rocket (sisymbrium austriacum)* / sisymbre d'autriche / cornacchia austriaca

"a shy stone not shying away—. . ."
> *bird's foot trefoil (lotus corniculatus)* / lotier corniculé / ginestrino

"your glance sends out a runner. . ."
> *creeping cinquefoil (potentilla reptans)* / potentille rampante (quintefeuille) / cinquefoglia comune

"like soft sage, this milky. . ."

> *jersey cudweed (helichrysum luteoalbum)* / gnaphale blanc jaunâtre /
> canapicchia pagliata

"shyly you put forth. . ."

> *meadow goat's beard (tragopogon pratensis)* / salsifis des prés / barba di
> becco dei prati

"you place your radiance. . ."

> *sunrose (helianthemum nummularium)* / hélianthème commun /
> eliantemo maggiore

"the droplets you hold. . ."

> *lady's mantle (alchemilla vulgaris)* / alchémille commune / alchemilla
> (erba stella)

"you never tear off. . ."

> *buckler-mustard (biscutella laevigata)* / lunetière lisse / biscutella
> montanina

"you bring bright stars. . ."

> *wood sorrel (oxalis)* / oxalis / oxalis

"your nipple-like buds. . ."

> *nipplewort (lapsana communis)* / lapsane commune / lassana grespignolo

"at your core a butterfly. . ."

> *alpine rock-cress (arabis alpina)* / arabette des Alpes / arabetta alpina

"whenever you hear. . ."

> *mouse-ear hawkweed (pilosella officinarum)* / épervière piloselle / sparviere
> pelosetto

"from your innermost whorl. . ."
　　pale madwort (alyssum alyssoides) / alysson à calices persistants / alisso annuo

"overlooked, neglected. . ."
　　st. james's wort (jacobaea vulgaris) / séneçon de jacob / senecione di san
　　giacomo

"unseen and when seen. . ."
　　toadflax (linaria supina) / linaire couchée / linajola dei serpentini

"vanquishing your restraint. . ."
　　honeysuckle (lonicera periclymenum) / chèvrefeuille / caprifoglio

"you are the nameless flower. . ."
　　nameless (sine nomine) / sans nom / senza nome

What Comes from the Night: three of these poems were first published in
The Bitter Oleander (Vol. 26, No. 2, Autumn 2020). The sentence quoted at
the end was found in Antonio Porchia's *Voces reunidas / Voix réunies,*
Toulouse, France: Éditions Eres, 2013, Fragment No. 523.

From What was Given: inspired by three tombstones on the wall of the
Saint-Gildas-de-Rhuys Abbey in Brittany.

To an Angel Depicted on a Reliquary: this sequence is based on a reliquary
found in the Notre-Dame de Cunault Church in the village of Cunault,
along the Loire River. After being published in *The Bitter Oleander* (Vol. 27,
No. 2, Autumn 2021), the poems were gathered in 2021 in a bibliophilic
chapbook, a limited edition produced by Estepa Editions and illustrated by
Kate Van Houten.

About the Author

John Taylor was born in Des Moines in 1952. He has lived in France since 1977. He is the author of several volumes of short prose and poetry, most recently *The Dark Brightness* (Xenos Books, 2017), *Grassy Stairways* (The MadHat Press, 2017), *Remembrance of Water & Twenty-Five Trees* (The Bitter Oleander Press, 2018), and a "double book" coauthored with the Swiss poet Pierre Chappuis, *A Notebook of Clouds & A Notebook of Ridges* (The Fortnightly Review Press, 2019). His first two books, *The Presence of Things Past* (Story Line Press, 1992) and *Mysteries of the Body and the Mind* (Story Line Press, 1998), were republished in new editions by Red Hen Press in 2020.

As a polyglot literary critic, Taylor has long been a bridge between European literature and English-speaking countries. His essays have been gathered by Transaction Publishers in his three-volume *Paths to Contemporary French Literature* (2004, 2007, 2011), *Into the Heart of European Poetry* (2008), and *A Little Tour through European Poetry* (2015).

Among his many translations of French, Italian, and Modern Greek literature are books by Philippe Jaccottet, Jacques Dupin, José-Flore Tappy, Pierre Voélin, Pierre Chappuis, Pierre-Albert Jourdan, Catherine Colomb, Pascal Quignard, Lorenzo Calogero, Alfredo de Palchi, Franca Mancinelli, Veroniki Dalakoura, and Elias Petropoulos. His translation of Elias Papadimitrakopoulos's stories, *Toothpaste with Chlorophyll & Maritime Hot Baths*, originally published by Asylum Arts in 1992, was republished in 2020 by Coyote Arts.

About the Illustrator

Sam Forder is a painter and draughtsman who lives and works near Cambridge, UK. He studied at Falmouth College of Art and The Royal Drawing School. His drawings are ultimately responsive to a lit moment whether sur le motif or in memory. His paintings manifest slowly over many months in the studio.

www.ingramcontent.com/pod-product-compliance
Lightning Source LLC
Chambersburg PA
CBHW031129020426
42333CB00012B/293